LeSSoNS
and
SuGGeSTioNS
FOR BUILDING
Your
Wealth

MARY BETH AND
NICHOLAS CLAPS

LESSONS
and
SUGGESTIONS
FOR BUILDING
Your
Wealth

MARY BETH AND
NICHOLAS CLAPS

Lessons and Suggestions for Building Your Wealth

Nicholas and Mary Beth Claps

F I R S T   E D I T I O N

Hardcover ISBN: 978-1-7363958-0-6
Paperback ISBN: 978-1-7363958-1-3
eBook ISBN: 978-1-7363958-2-0

Library of Congress Control Number: 2020925834

NSP
Nebraska Sower Press

The information in this book is neither intended nor implied to be a substitute
for professional, financial, or legal advice. All content is for general educational
purposes only. The authors are not certified financial planners/advisors and make
no representations and assume no responsibility for the accuracy or efficacy of the
information herein and shall have no liability for any damages or loss from reliance on
the information herein.

To our parents,
who gave us the tools to build our success.

To our nineteen nieces and nephews who,
through the years, have given us love and joyful memories.

To all future generations,
in the hope that this book gives you
a head start in the right direction.

Contents

INTRODUCTION

WE WISH SOMEONE HAD TOLD US THESE THINGS.

We are in our seventies, enjoying fulfilling and active lives. We feel fortunate to have shared many good times and are thankful for our memories. We've had lots of experiences—some good and some not. As a result, we have learned many valuable life lessons. *These are things we wish someone had told us early in life.*

We hope that the **lessons** and **suggestions** contained in this book can, in some way, benefit and empower our nephews, nieces, family members, and others for generations to come.

In 1992, we decided to establish a scholarship in our names at the University of Nebraska Foundation (Nicholas J. and Mary B. Claps Scholarship, dated 2/22/1992) since we did not have any children of our own. When the scholarship was established, we hoped it might benefit our nineteen nieces and nephews and other students from our area of New York.

1

We established the scholarship at a relatively early age in case we met untimely deaths. As fate would have it, we are enjoying long lives. Therefore, we hope our scholarship will benefit future generations since it will not be funded until after our deaths. However, our scholarship is accepting donations and we ask that you consider giving to it so it will continue to benefit future generations.

Love,

Mary Beth and Nick Claps

BEGINNING

Love is the strongest and most powerful force in the world. We wrote this book to lovingly share things no one ever explained to us. We intend for this material to help all our nieces and nephews. Throughout the years, we have learned that others want to know this information as well; this is why we decided to write this book.

The book contains both **lessons** and **suggestions**. **Lessons** are things that are basic and will never change. For example, one plus one equals two, money grows in a curve, and income minus expenses equals discretionary dollars or debt (negative money). **Suggestions** are choices; these are up to you. If you are married, you and your spouse will have to decide what is right for both of you. Remember, your choices will affect you throughout your life.

For example, say you need a new computer. You have a choice between a computer that meets all your needs or another one with extras that you like that is much more expensive. That choice is the same for a vehicle. Do you buy a costly vehicle or not? Both vehicles will get you from point A to B. The choice is yours.

Our choices are important. *The Millionaire Next Door*[1], a compilation of research on the profiles of millionaires, points out how important choices are. Go to your library and get the audio-book.

This is your life, and how you travel through it will be up to you. Saving money along the way gives you more choices throughout life, especially in retirement. We want you to have a healthy financial life without money worries. That is the point of this book—to help you achieve a life without money worries.

To build a better understanding of life, we suggest reading various books or watching movies about different peoples' lives. This book is based on our experiences, as well as the conditions and laws at the time of its publication. By the time you read it, some things will have changed. Find ways to work with them, around them, or through them. Have fun as you do it. *Following the lessons and suggestions in this book almost guarantees you will become a millionaire.*

We tried to write this so a very young person—anyone ten and older—could use the information. We hope the lessons and suggestions will help you. If they do, please pass them onto your children, grandchildren, nieces, and nephews.

---

[1]   Thomas J. Stanley and William D. Danko, *The Millionaire Next Door: The Surprising Secrets of America's Wealthy* (Taylor Trade Publishing, 1996).

LESSON: SAVE MONEY

Saving money should begin as early as possible. Why? Because you will have a lot of money throughout your life.

Consider two kids, ages ten and twelve, who sweep garages and pick up sticks and branches that have fallen from trees. They make up a flyer on their computer and pass it out in their neighborhood:

> We sweep garages, moving items away from the surrounding walls and cleaning behind those items we can move. We charge $10 per garage.
>
> We pick up sticks and branches that have fallen from trees in your yard so you can use your mower safely and without causing damage to the mower. We charge $5 per wheelbarrow of brush.
>
> Call us, Tony and John at (999) 999-9999. If we do not answer, please leave your name and phone number.

This is only one example of things kids can do to earn money at a young age. Nick swept neighbors' garages, shoveled driveways in the winter, raked leaves during the fall, mowed lawns, etc., to earn money. Use your imagination to think of services that you can provide. The only person preventing you from earning money is you!

Use your imagination to find, do, and create work

If you want to earn money, it is out there. Go for it! The internet is full of ideas. Try different word searches. Some suggestions include

- Jobs you can do without leaving the house
- Best jobs for kids under thirteen
- Best part-time jobs to make extra money

As you move from elementary school to middle school to high school to college or trade school, find something you can do part-time to earn money and keep saving. Even part-time work will help your savings grow.

If a ten-year-old consistently saves half of all the money he receives from birthdays, allowances, working for others (e.g., cleaning garages), while enjoying spending the other half of the money, he will be financially secure at a very early age. This is what saving can do for you.

Why do you think there are programs to help save for retirement that do not allow you to touch the money until you are 59½? These allow you to have money at retirement. However, many people fail to start saving until they are fifty or older. That is sad.

Save half and enjoy the other half, but start saving money. You will become a millionaire. How? See the graph in the next lesson to watch how money grows. Many people, even smart ones, are not aware of this. If they were, everyone would start saving money the day they receive his or her first allowance.

LESSON: MONEY GROWS IN A CURVE

This graph best illustrates how money grows—on a curve rather than a straight line.

This growth happens wherever you deposit your money, including savings accounts, money market accounts, CD accounts, stock mutual funds, etc.

YOUR MONEY GROWS FOR YOU, WITHOUT YOU DOING ANYTHING TO ACHIEVE THAT GROWTH

For example, $100 deposited in a savings account earning 3 percent interest will grow $3 by the end of one year—$3 you did not have to work for. You can just sit around watching TV as your money grows.

Understanding this makes the difference between a rich person and a poor person who spends all their money rather than saving any. By always saving some money whenever you earn, you will never have to worry about money later in life.

Do you want to be financially secure at thirty or forty? Never touch the money you save, and get on the curve to an easy life. Life can be good without worrying about money.

SUGGESTION: THINK ABOUT THE LONG-TERM IMPACT OF YOUR CHOICES

Why is this a suggestion? You must live below your means to save money; it's a choice. *The Millionaire Next Door* is one of our favorite books for better understanding the impact different choices can have.

For example, let's say you're shopping for a backpack for school. Do you need a designer, monogrammed, all-leather backpack with special pockets that costs $500, or do you need a simple, durable, fabric backpack with a couple of pockets that costs $48? Both will carry your belongings. The choice is yours. Which backpack do you choose?

As another example, you need a vehicle to get to work. Do you buy an inexpensive, reliable vehicle or a high-end, expensive vehicle? The choice is yours. Both vehicles will get you to and from work. Which will you choose?

SUGGESTION: START SAVING WHEN YOU ARE VERY YOUNG

This suggestion is for anyone who wants to reward themselves with a comfortable life sooner rather than later.

If you can start saving 50 percent of everything you earn at a very young age and never spend that money, you could be a millionaire before age thirty-nine. As a guest on NBC's *The Willie Geist Show*, Shaquille O'Neal said that the super-rich would save 75 percent and only spend 25 percent of what they made so they could get rich faster.

We enjoyed life but also saved some money as we earned it, and by the time Nick was thirty-five, we were financially secure. We always held jobs that provided the income to maintain our standard of living. However, our financial security at an early age was made possible by finding ways to earn additional income.

If you want to work, work is out there. Either develop a side job or find someone who needs extra help, even for a short time. The opportunity to earn extra money is always out there. You just have to find it or develop a need for it yourself.

If you have your own business, you can deduct many different items from your income, whether the business made a profit or lost money. The losses can be subtracted from other income posted on your taxes. This is a good way of using the tax code to help keep more of your money. We recommend the book *Deduct It! Lower Your Small Business Taxes*[2] to better understand taxes and owning a business.

---

[2]   Stephen Fishman, *Deduct It! Lower Your Small Business Taxes* (Nolo Books)

INSPIRATION #1

NEVER GIVE UP. NEVER GIVE UP. No one is perfect; just try to make the best of every situation and turn obstacles into learning opportunities. BE PERSISTENT.

LESSON: THERE ARE ONLY THREE MAIN PLACES TO PUT MONEY: CASH, BONDS, AND STOCKS

Examples of each:

- Cash: Checking and savings accounts, CDs, money market accounts, etc.
- Bonds: Corporate bonds, municipal bonds, EE bonds, I bonds, international bonds, etc.
- Stocks: Individual stocks, mutual funds, international stocks, exchange-traded funds (ETFs), etc.

Research "financial planning." The more knowledge you have about finances, the better you will understand your financial plan. Working with a financial planner will allow you to understand your finances even better.

Below is an example of how to allocate your money in cash, bonds, and stocks at different ages.

Age	Cash	Bonds	Stocks	Total
25–55	15 percent	10 percent	75 percent	**100 percent**
55–70	20 percent	20 percent	60 percent	**100 percent**
70–100	30 percent	30 percent	40 percent	**100 percent**

As you get closer to retirement (about seven to ten years before retiring), have all dividends and capital gains sent to your portfolio's money market to keep building cash before you retire.

All the above percentages will change based on how much risk you can take (tolerate) when the stock market goes up and down. Remember, you need *cash* to buy things. That is why you will read "cash is king" in some financial books, especially when times are bad. However, your needs should be less than your cash flow (i.e., salary, wages, interest, etc.).

All interest, dividends, and capital gains were automatically deposited in our money market. This made retirement easy since cash was piling up on its own. We only had to spend it. We never worried about the 2008 market crash or the effect of the coronavirus pandemic on the economy. This is the type of retirement you want. Just play and have fun, like you did as a kid. Don't worry about money; all your money is on autopilot.

LESSON: UNDERSTAND DOLLAR COST AVERAGING

Save your money weekly, monthly, or quarterly through a 401K plan, payroll deduction plan, or your own plan.

Wherever you place your dollars (e.g., S&P 500 Index Fund), you will be buying shares at all different prices. Sometimes your share prices will be high (up), and other times, your share prices will be low (down), but on average, your cost for each share will be less. This is what dollar cost averaging is all about.

(*Note: Two suggestions for companies to invest in the S&P 500 Index Fund are: Fidelity 800-343-3548 Fidelity 500 Index Fund [call letters FXAIX] Vanguard 877-662-7447 Vanguard 500 Index Fund Admiral Shares [call letters VFIAX]*)

LESSON: INVEST IN CAPITALISM

Capitalism is an economic and political system in which a country's trade and industry are controlled by private owners for profit, rather than by the state.

When driving a car, you know how to use the steering wheel, the gas pedal, and brake. You do not understand how the engine or transmission work, but you still can drive. So it is with our complex economic system. You don't need to be an economist to participate.

One way to do so is to purchase the S&P 500 Index Fund. Start by investing in the fund and then learn more about the markets. We'll talk more about the S&P 500 Index fund later.

LESSON AND SUGGESTION: KEEP A BUDGET

Some people say, "We will never live on a budget; we spend as we please." However, everyone lives on a budget. Everyone must pay specific bills like rent/mortgage, utilities, car loans, etc.

Keeping a budget on paper is very important, but it is a choice. Making a list of budget items does take effort.[3] However, this list will help you make future decisions and shows you how money can accumulate.

For example, you have set aside $95 in your budget to go out every Friday night. However, for some unexpected reason, you need money for something else. You can look at your budget and decide to eat out every *other* Friday, which will give you an extra $190 each month.

---

[3] This site will help you get started: *https://www.tiaa.org/public/learn/personal-finance-101/how-to-make-a-budget.* To see examples of a budget, search "budget templates" online.

Another example: After you pay off your auto loan of $500/month, you can keep saving the $500/month toward your next vehicle, or you can keep $250/month in the auto budget and use the other $250/month to purchase something you need for the household (e.g., new stove, TV, coffee maker, etc.). Having a budget on paper will help make those decisions.

LESSON: YOU ARE ON A TIMELINE

You are on a timeline, whether you like it or not. Life goes on.

Putting your timeline on paper gives you a picture/sense of what is ahead of you. A timeline can help you see the future more clearly as you add items to it, such as the ages of family members, when children will be going to college, when you want to retire, etc.

The following table provides an example of a timeline:

People & Ages	2020	2025	2030	2035	2040	2045	2050	2055
Daughter, 5				College	Possible wedding			
Son, 10			College	Possible wedding				
Spouse, 34			Age 44	Age 49				
You, 35			Age 45	Age 50			Age 65	
					Possible grandkids		Early retirement	
							Selling the house?	

This timeline shows what ages you and your spouse will be when each child is in college, possibly getting married, having children, etc. The timeline can help decide how long you stay in your current home and how to save for college expenses, wedding expenses, retirement, etc. It can show you when to downsize, what the children and grandchildren are doing, what other properties you might want to buy and when, or when to sell properties (e.g., a camp, ski lodge, boats, etc.). All this information helps with planning and decision-making.[4]

---

[4] For more information, research "how to plan for a successful future" or similar searches on the internet.

SUGGESTION:
KEEP YOUR TAXES LOW

There are many ways to lower your taxes. As you earn and save money, start thinking about how to pay less in taxes. You can place your money into sheltered instruments like annuities, 401K plans, IRAs, etc. Speak to a financial planner[5] to learn more about sheltering your money from taxes or search "sheltering your money from taxes" on the internet.

Another way to possibly pay lower taxes is by starting your own side business. For example, if you work in the IT sector, you can help others remotely. You could charge based on time or per project. You could also turn a hobby into a side business. For example, you enjoy painting nature scenes and decide to start a small business selling your paintings. A painting you display at an art show sells for $125. The cost of the painting

---

[5] If you use a financial planner, make sure you clearly understand the fees charged.

to you was $25, earning you $100. The side business may be something you will continue to enjoy doing even during your retirement years. You can have fun and lower your taxes at the same time!

Having a small business generates deductions. When you work for and are paid by an employer, you have no deductions. You cannot deduct the vehicle you drive back and forth to work. However, if you have a side business of your own, you can deduct a portion of the vehicle. Other items may also be deductible, such as cell phones, tools, books, etc.

The book *Deduct It!: Lower Your Small Business Taxes*[6] will help you find all the things you can deduct to lower your taxes. Use a tax preparer, too. You'll get good advice and guidance from both, helping you save more money.

---

[6] Stephen Fishman, *Nolo Books*

SUGGESTION: KNOW THE LAW

Small claims court is one of the legal system's resources you should be familiar with. Why? It is much cheaper to represent yourself for small claims of $5,000 or less (amount varies) than hiring a lawyer. Every person has the right to represent him or herself in a court of law.[7] The difficulty with the law is understanding its procedures.

Some small business owners have difficulty collecting their money after completing services. For example, a landscaper performs a job and does not want to have problems collecting payment from the customer. What can she do?

If you have a side business, you should have a contract with each of your customers before you do business with them. In your contract, be specific about what you will do and what

---

[7] A good reference for this subject is the book *Everybody's Guide to Small Claims Court* by Cara O'Neill, Nolo Books).

your customer will do, including how you will collect payment. For example, after half the job is completed, the customer will pay you half of the total. Then, if you end up having to go to court, you only have to sue for a smaller amount of money. Suing does take time, but sometimes that knowledge about the law and contracts can help you become more effective.

Here's a sample contract[8]:

I (your name) agree to:

- *Plant 21 plants,*
- *Place landscaping fabric around plants and open areas of landscaping, and*
- *Finish off with mulch.*

I will be paid $2,100 for the complete work in the following installments:

- *After the first day of work and inspection by Mr. and Mrs. Jones, $700 cash will be paid (receipt will be given).*
- *After half of the work on the landscaping has been done and inspected by Mr. and Mrs. Jones, another $700 cash will be paid (receipt will be given).*
- *After the landscaping job is completed and inspected by Mr. and Mrs. Jones, the last $700 cash will be paid (receipt will be given).*

Mr. and Mrs. Jones will provide:

- *21 plants,*
- *3 roles of landscaping fabric, and*
- *8 yards of mulch (see order form 4589 at Home Depot).*

They will pay me $2,100 for my services in three easy installments.

Sign and date contract.

---

[8]   For more information, search "What are the elements of a contract?" on the internet.

You can also use small claims court if you disagree with a contractor who is working on your house. Just be sure you have a detailed contract signed and dated by both parties before work begins.

Remember, our whole world is made up of laws; we all follow the laws whether we like them or not. These laws are the rules of the game, the "Game of Life." If you know the rules that affect your life and can use them to your advantage, you can play the game the best you can.

LESSON: LIFE IS A GAME

Millionaires and billionaires sometimes say, "Life is a game. How you play the game will get you to where you want to be, and the money will follow."

An investor on TV said, "We do it for the love of the game, and if you do it well, the money will follow."

Why do we say life is a game? When we think about life as a game, we enjoy the game. And we do what we can to do well in the game.

A good work ethic is one of the keys to doing well in the game. For us, this meant doing quality work, being on time, staying longer than we were asked to, and being courteous and considerate. Our parents taught us this.

For example, a contractor who loves his work gives 100 percent attention to each project and corrects all mistakes without being asked because he loves what he does and does it well. He does it so well that people appreciate him for it and tell others. More people want the same—that is how the money follows.

Play the game and play it well.

LESSON: WHO ARE YOU?

You are different, and there is no one else like you.
You become who you want to be.
You become the product of all the things around you.
Keep doing the things that you enjoy and make you happy.
Look at life as something to cherish with your loved ones.
Make your life easy and fun,
and enjoy the beauty of your surroundings.
Take time to appreciate what is good in your life.
You are different, and there is no one else like you.

SUGGESTION: IMPROVE YOUR STATUS

If you feel discouraged because you are unable to get a good job, are stuck in a dead-end job, are unemployed and living in a run-down neighborhood, or have some other problem(s), then take action. *You are the only one who can begin to improve your life/status and "get on the curve."*

Try to find some way to earn extra cash for you and your family through a side business (i.e., offering services people may need like cleaning, mowing, etc.). All the extra cash you make should go into a savings account. When you have enough saved, open an S&P 500 Index Fund through Vanguard or Fidelity and keep adding to that fund whenever you can. Have all dividends and capital gains sent to your money market. Your money market will be your extra cash for emergencies, taxes, and retirement savings.

As a reminder, never touch the money you have in the S&P 500 Index Fund. The value will go up and down, but in time, you will have more money than you had before. Do NOT let the fear of a down market scare you to sell. This value (money) will come back, and you will be happy you waited. To learn more, talk to any financial professional on the phone for free and learn from them. Also, read about the ups and downs of the market. Finally, see the special section toward the end of this book called "Your Business."

Get working and saving and use the lessons and suggestions in this book. If your actions and efforts help you improve your status and situation and you become successful, please consider donating to our scholarship (details are at the end of the book).

INSPIRATION #2

If you are saving money and putting it in the bank and then into the S&P 500 Index Fund, you will see how your money makes you money for doing nothing. You are getting yourself on the curve. You can accomplish anything you set your mind to!

LESSON:
BE WISE ABOUT DEBT

You should never be in debt until you have secured steady employment in your chosen field. Until then, save and buy only the things you need, not want. When you have a more permanent job, you can take out a loan to buy a house or a vehicle.

Never, ever have credit card debt. Always pay off 100 percent of your credit card debt each month when you receive your statement. If you cannot do this, do not have credit cards; otherwise, you will be in debt to the credit card company for life. The worst debt you can have is credit card debt that rolls over each month, because you will pay very high interest rates on this debt—a **losing game for you** and a **winning game for the credit card company**. This is the same for any installment payment plan, so beware of the temptation of instant gratification.

A credit card may cause you to give in to instant gratification because it facilitates impulse buying. This is the bad side of having a credit card, especially when you get that "I want it now" feeling. Impulse buying does not allow you to determine whether the purchase is a need or a want. Sometimes waiting is the best thing you can do to make wise financial decisions.

Try what's known as the "Ben Franklin Method." Draw a line down the center of a piece of paper. Label one side NEED and the other side WANT. In each column, list why you either need or want the item. If you want something simply to show off to others, you know it is not a need. This exercise will show you whether you need to make the purchase.

Dave Ramsey's book, *The Total Money Makeover: A Proven Plan for Financial Fitness*[9] will help you better understand debt and how companies try to make you poor.

---

[9] Ramsey, Dave, *The Total Money Makeover: A Proven Plan for Financial Fitness* (Thomas Nelson).

LESSON: FIGHT CREDIT CARD COMPANY ERRORS IMMEDIATELY

Sometimes, credit card companies make mistakes and erroneously charge you a late fee and interest, both at high rates. The battle to correct this mistake can take months, a year, or even more, so contact the credit card company immediately about the error.

Here's how to solve the problem. To begin with, you should have at least two credit cards. Do not make any additional transactions on the credit card that has the error until the error is corrected. Immediately start using only the other credit card. If the credit card with an error has any automatic payments, be sure to have them stopped.

Send a letter to the credit card company explaining the mistake. Make sure you have copies of everything you send to the credit card company, and create a file with the statement that has the error. This will help you establish a good paper trail regarding the credit card company's error. Include all written correspondence you receive or send, as well as notes of any phone calls. These notes should include the name, phone number, and extension of the person you speak with, as well as the date, time, and a record of everything discussed with that individual.

If the company does not correct the error immediately, stop using that credit card. Be sure to pay *all* the charges you legally made, but do not pay any erroneous fees, interest, late charges, etc. When you have a statement with only fees, late charges, etc., return this statement with a letter stating that all of your legally obligated charges have been paid and that the fees, interest, and other charges are due to the credit card company's mistake.

The credit card company will keep sending you statements each month, saying, "You must pay." With each monthly statement, return a copy of your letter that explains why the credit card company is in error. Make sure to keep a copy in your file.

Notice how fast the late charges, fees, interest, etc., add up. Scary, huh?

After six months, send the credit card company one last letter stating that you have paid all your legal obligations and enclose a copy of your past correspondences, stating that this *will be your last letter to them.* In the letter, tell the credit card company to take you to court if they think you are wrong. Send the letter by certified mail, and use the tracking number to see when the credit card company receives your letter. Print a copy of the website page showing the date of delivery and place the copy in your file. You might not hear from the credit card company again.

However, later on, you might get a letter from a collection company. Dispute it on your credit report, if it shows up there, and send the credit report company a copy of the last letters you sent to the credit card company. Be sure you can answer the following questions if the matter ever does go before a judge:

- Can you clearly show the credit card company's mistake?

- Can you show that you paid all your bills on time each month?

- Can you show the only reason you had fees, late charges, interest, etc., was due to the credit card company's error?

If you can answer yes to these questions, then you should win the case.

LESSON FROM WARREN BUFFET

Warren Buffet said that if he died before his wife, all their money should be placed in the S&P 500 Index Fund at Vanguard because the fund outperformed 90 percent of all other funds. Why would Warren Buffett tell his widow to buy an index fund?

The S&P 500 Index Fund has good diversification with 500 different companies. It gives both dividends and capital gains.

Throughout the years, various publications have explained that most investors are better off buying low-cost mutual funds, such as the S&P 500 Index Fund. Most companies and the vast majority of active mutual-fund managers fail to outperform the broader stock market over time. Over fifteen years, about 92 percent of large-cap funds trailed the S&P, according to some reports. Additionally, as many as 95 percent of fund managers trying to beat indexes for medium-sized companies trail their benchmark indices.

LESSON: BUILDING YOUR WEALTH WILL GIVE YOU CHOICES

Financial independence/security is empowering. When you have financial independence, you can work because you want to work, not because you have to. *That is a choice.* You realize you have this inner power, that you can always find another position/job. You can only get that feeling of power when you are financially secure. This empowerment gives you an inner feeling of pride, one that says, "I am here working because I *want* to be here, not because I have to."

LESSON: TEACH YOUR CHILDREN TO SOLVE PROBLEMS

Showing your children how to solve problems independently is one of the best things you can do to help them. When your child asks you for something and you always buy it for them, you hurt yourself and the child.

Since we didn't have children of our own, our friends "Mr. and Mrs. Brown" helped us with this lesson. Their names have been changed to respect their wishes; they do not want their children or other family members to know that they have built over $8 million of wealth.

Mrs. and Mr. Brown had six children, and they told us, "You cannot help six kids on our income. You have to give them the skills to solve problems on their own. This way, they can be independent throughout life."

This lesson is essential. Knowing how to solve problems is

a good life skill, and being able to do more on your own will help you in life. As early as you can, you should give children problems to solve on their own. For example, maybe at six months, take a favorite toy of the child and, in front of the child, place the toy in a paper bag and close it. Then, give the bag to the child and see what the child does. The goal is for the child to rip open the paper bag and take the toy out. This helps develop problem-solving skills at an early age.

Another important problem-solving skill to help your child develop is decision-making related to needs and wants. For example, your child wants to buy something with her own money that she received on her birthday as a gift. Whatever she wants to buy, this is a good time for you, as the parent, to have a helpful discussion with her about making choices based **on needs and wants.**

As mentioned, the Browns had six children to feed and clothe. Their children learned to solve their problems rather than depend on their parents to help them in every situation. When one child asked if he could buy a vehicle, the parents said, "Yes, just figure it out on your own." They did give this child a suggestion to start looking for a part-time job.

At the time of this writing, our friends have more money than we do. Why are we telling you this? Many people have the misconception that wealth can only be built when you don't have children. But this is incorrect; the key to becoming wealthy is to learn how to save.

LESSON: IF YOU HAVE A FINANCIAL PLANNER, ASK ABOUT HIS OR HER FEES

Years ago, financial planners made money in two ways. They received commissions on products sold, such as life insurance or investments that had a commission.

You might be surprised how much financial planners collect today. A financial planner will have you sign a contract to pay an ongoing fee no matter whether you make or lose money.

Two of our friends did not know what fees they were paying their financial planners. One friend learned he was paying $14,000 per year. After five years, he had paid his financial planner $70,000 for two planning sessions per year. In each session, his planner said, "Everything looks good; stay the course." He found another planner with the same services for half the price.

The other friend was pretty smart. She knew that financial planners charge a percentage based on the amount of money they manage, so she split her money in half. Her planner managed $250,000 of her money, while she self-managed the other $250,000. This way, she had a professional to talk to and someone to bounce questions off. This situation forced her to read more and get more involved in her finances. After eight years, she felt she could handle her finances completely.

HINT

No one knows when an economic storm will happen; not even the best professionals.

Economic storms are inevitable. They will come in different forms. Therefore, have a healthy supply of cash to get through any storm. When the storm ends and good economic times have returned, you should check your investments. From the investments that have increased in value, sell some shares, and move the money to your cash position. Now you are ready for the next economic storm. Good luck.

SUGGESTION: YOU GROW INTO RETIREMENT, JUST AS YOU GREW INTO YOUR JOB (CAREER/WORK)

During your working years, you grow into your job, even if you change jobs. You learn new skills, develop your work habits, and grow into a better you. You want to learn as much as you can for work.

Additionally, you are always making decisions related to home and family during these years. Since you have a vehicle and a house, you want to learn handyman skills to complete little jobs around the house and to maintain your vehicle. Every job you can do yourself saves you money.

For example, from an article about WD-40, we learned that spraying WD-40 on your vehicle battery terminals prevents corrosion. Therefore, as soon as we purchased a new vehicle, we would spray the battery terminals to prevent corrosion and extend the battery's life. This one hint saved us a lot of money on batteries and maintained our batteries' cranking power.

During retirement, you start to develop a new routine. Take time to prioritize what is important, as well as doing the things you enjoy. As you learn more about yourself, you may even find that what is important also changes.

For example, you may look around your house and find many things that you no longer need or use. Cleaning out this stuff is a process that will help you simplify your life.

You will be better able to focus on what is important to you. This may include learning about proper nutrition, along with good food preparation methods. You may enjoy being more active, spending time outdoors, catching up on reading, traveling, etc. During retirement, you have the time to play with your grandchildren and pass some of your skills and knowledge on to them and others in the younger generation.

When you have no money worries in retirement, it gives you more free time to do the things that make you happy. You grow into retirement.

NOTE ON THE NEXT THREE LESSONS

- Taking money out of the markets is like taking water from a well.

- Take dividends and gains from your investments and hold them in cash.

- You'll be both happy and sad when you sell your shares.

These lessons are interrelated because the bottom line is having a good cash position before you retire.

LESSON: TAKING MONEY OUT OF THE MARKETS IS LIKE TAKING WATER FROM A WELL

Especially in your retirement years, take money out of the markets even if you do not need it. A good way to think about this is to use a well as an example.

During a dry season, you notice that the water level in your well went down. You decide to have a backup system for when your water level is low. During a rainy season, you notice the water level in your well is high. You decide to take extra water from the well and add it to your backup system. This way, you always have a good amount of water and never have to worry about a dry season again.

This is what you should do during your retirement years with the money in your S&P 500 Index Fund account and your money market account. You have been saving money in the S&P 500 Index Fund account for several years and have never touched/used this money. The value of the S&P 500 Index Fund account is $100,000; this will be the benchmark.

When the S&P 500 Index Fund account value is $110,000, take $10,000 out and send it to your money market account. Do not touch your S&P 500 Index Fund account until it gets up to $110,000 again. Then, take $10,000 from your S&P 500 Index Fund account and send it to your money market account again. If for some reason the S&P 500 Index Fund account value goes to $115,000, still take out $10,000, and leave the other $5,000 in the account.

As time goes on, your money market account has grown by $30,000, and you should have about $100,000 in your S&P 500 Index Fund account. You may not need more cash from your S&P 500 Index Fund account for several years, but as it grows, you have a place to get cash if you need it.

Stop taking money from your S&P 500 Index Fund account when you feel you have enough money in cash (in your money market account). This amount might be different for different people. You might feel comfortable with just the amount of cash you need to cover your budget, or you might feel as if you need three to four times that amount. It depends on your comfort level Or, you could decide that when your S&P 500 Index Fund account is valued at $250,000, you plan to take another $10,000, or that when your S&P 500 Index Fund account is valued at $300,000, you plan to take another $20,000. This is only a game, and you make your own rules, so enjoy yourself.

LESSON: TAKE DIVIDENDS AND GAINS FROM YOUR INVESTMENTS AND HOLD THEM IN CASH

You should be building your cash position many years before retirement. Do not wait until you are 100 percent retired; you will never find the perfect time to sell your shares of stock (we call it "The Happy/Sad Case"; see the next lesson). Start taking all dividends and capital gains from your investments and have them sent to your money market. That way, your cash position builds up automatically, and you will have a healthy cash position when retirement comes. You will always love having cash around, especially when hard times hit, such as the Great Recession of 2008 and the coronavirus pandemic. This is when "cash is king."

LESSON: YOU'LL BE HAPPY AND SAD WHEN YOU SELL YOUR SHARES

During retirement, no time is perfect to sell shares of stock. However, you have to sell those shares to have cash. Remember, you cannot buy things with Apple stock, but you can buy anything you like once you turn your stock into cash.

When you sell your shares at a higher price than you bought them, you are very happy. You are even happier after selling your shares at a high when the market drops the next day. You think you are a genius.

However, when you sold your shares and they go up again the next day, you feel sad. That is the nature of the game. So get over it, and look at the bright side—you have cash in your pocket, and when you die, you cannot take any of this stuff with you.

LESSON: YOU SHOULD NOT GIVE LARGE AMOUNTS OF MONEY TO YOUR LOVED ONES

This might be difficult to understand. However, many of you will better understand it as you get older.

When anyone is just *given* money—especially large sums—they often do not handle it well. When someone *earns* those same dollars, they have a vested interest in that money, and their thinking about how they handle it is quite different. They are unlikely to feel "easy come, easy go."

When you work hard for your money, you usually value it more and make wiser decisions. Many times, more harm than good comes from giving a person too much money.

LESSON: WATCH OUT FOR THE "CON"

How much savings you have is no one else's business. Keep your finances/savings to yourself, and do not tell anyone you have money. People will play on your heart and try to soften you up with a sad song. Someone will always be trying to get your money.

It can be anybody—family, friend, or stranger. But you are not their bank.

Some red flags to watch for are:

- When someone needs your money or wants to borrow your money.

- When someone tells you, "This will be the best investment you will ever make!"

Be careful out there.

LESSON: PLAN FOR OLD AGE

Chances are, you will live until you are very old.[10] Therefore, you should plan for old age.

Once you are married and have children, you should get a term life insurance policy[11] in the unlikely chance you die early. The policy term should be for 20 years. Then, save money and plan to live a very long time. Do not let any insurance person scare you and make you buy a very expensive policy with very little life insurance.

---

[10] Do an internet search for "life expectancy" for more information.

[11] Compare the cost of a term life insurance policy with the cost of a regular life insurance policy. Names for other regular life insurance policies include "whole life," "universal life," "variable life," etc.

SUGGESTION: READ A VARIETY OF BOOKS

Reading books will help in many ways. Reading a variety of books will help you develop greater problem-solving skills and will help with real life experiences. It will help you learn about other points of view and make you a more well-rounded person, able to better connect with others. Some recommendations are:

- Warren Buffet books
- Ruth Bader Ginsburg books
- *The Wisdom of Finance: Discovering Humanity in the World of Risk and Return* by Mihir A. Desai
- *Principles: Life and Work* by Ray Dalio
- *What It Takes: Lessons in the Pursuit of Excellence* by Stephen Schwarzman
- *How to Win Friends and Influence People* by Dale Carnegie

- *Up From Nothing* by John Hope Bryant
- Science books
- Math books

LESSON: SHOULD I HAVE PRIVATE HOLDINGS?

Many wealthy people invest in private holdings. Why? Usually, multimillionaires like to talk about their unique holdings at parties and other types of get togethers.

The downside is selling the private holding. The market can be small, and selling that private holding can take a lot of time. Therefore, stay with your main investments like the S&P 500 Index Fund, even if you have $10 million.

INSPIRATION #3

If you are ten or older, you should read this book now and again during your retirement. As you have various life experiences, your thinking and ideas change.

Focus on the positive.

Believe in yourself.

Enjoy life to the fullest.

LESSON: CHANGES HAPPEN AS WE AGE

Our parents and grandparents often did not say much about their physical or cognitive issues that emerged as they aged. Why? One reason might have been that they felt we, as the children, did not have the skillset to help them. Perhaps they did not want us to worry about them, or they may have been embarrassed about their issues. Or, they may have felt we had other problems to attend to.

How can you help? Where do you become important? You can make sure the system (Medicare) is working for your parents and taking care of them. You can make sure they are getting the medical attention they need. Take notice of whether they are becoming forgetful or seem to be easily confused. They also may need assistance handling their finances.

The last stage in life is dying. We all must die sometime. Children need to talk to their parents to support their wishes at the end of life.

SUGGESTION: SHOULD YOU OWN A HOUSE IN RETIREMENT?

This is a difficult decision with no right or wrong answer. What lifestyle do you want?

This was our decision: In retirement, we planned to travel south for the winter months. Later, we decided to move to a southern state. The hunt was on for where to live. We traveled along the east coast from Virginia to the Florida Keys to find a location. Along the way, we had fun and gained a good education about our country.

After finding what we thought was a good spot, we sold our home and rented a condo in New York to downsize in order to relocate with suitcases only. We planned to build a new house with new furniture, etc. We rented a condo in Florida while searching for a location and a builder for our new home.

However, during that time, we met and talked with a cross section of retirees in Florida. From what we learned, we decided that living in Florida was not right for us.

We also decided that homeownership was not right for us. Owning a house comes with many responsibilities we did not want anymore. As we aged, we realized we no longer wanted to do things like routine maintenance, repairs, managing contractors, etc. We wanted everything to be taken care of without any responsibilities. That is what living in our condo complex gave us.

Owning a home is the right decision for some people. A home could be the most reasonable and/or desirable place to live. For example, your home is paid off (no mortgage or loans against the house), and you only have your taxes and maintenance and repair expenses to pay.

We also realized we had overlooked all the advantages of living in central New York. The area has beautiful weather in spring, summer (low humidity), and fall. Winters were problematic for us, mainly January and February, but traveling would solve this problem.

Another advantage of living in central New York is its proximity to many places, such as New York City, the Finger Lakes, the Adirondacks, Thousand Islands, the Great Lakes, Canada, etc. Finally, another great advantage is the reasonable cost of living.

We share this to show that decision-making is a process. If you change a major decision, be sure you have clear, sound reasons for making that change. The question to ask yourself is "What is good for me/us?" Depending on what you enjoy, the choice is yours. Have joy in your life. Make it what you want.

SUGGESTION: BUILD YOUR OWN MONEY MACHINE

You need to place your money where it can earn a return (it must be money you do not plan to spend for a long time). This will help your money grow on that upward curve, hopefully early in your life.

To build your own money machine is a choice. If you save as early as possible and spend like the "Millionaire Next Door," you will find that your overall income will be much higher than what you spend. This is when your life becomes most enjoyable.

For us, it was when Nick stopped working at forty-eight. To clarify, he stopped formal work and started doing things he enjoyed the most. We had all dividends, interest, and capital gains sent to our money market accounts to build cash. Nick was doing occasional work that he enjoyed. Mary Beth continued teaching until retiring at age fifty-five.

As we aged, we turned more and more of our money into cash. We ended up with so much cash we could not spend it all.

Let us clarify this point—any fool can spend all their money. For example, many people have come into a sudden windfall (i.e., winning a $10 million lottery) and then spent all that money in a short period, leaving them right back where they started.

The more cash we had, the more worry-free we were. The more we could act like kids (no worries), the more fun we had. This was our goal, and this life gave us great enjoyment. Our money machine let us travel the world, travel every winter, treat our relatives and friends, and gave us 100 percent freedom. We hope you get to build your own money machine to enjoy whatever your dreams may be.

SPECIAL SECTION: YOUR BUSINESS

If you plan to have your own business, there are a few things to consider about your business's name. If you have a clever name you want to use (e.g., Mr. Flowers), you must go to your county and determine whether anyone is using that name. If so, you need a new name. If not, you need to file a DBA ("doing business as") and pay a fee to register your name. This means no one else can use that name but you.

If you do not want to file for a DBA, you can use your name as the company name. Since your name is you, no one can use your name. For example, if your name is John W. Jones, your business could be "John W. Jones – we do landscaping," or "John W. Jones – we do painting," etc.

We recommend Nolo books to help with running your business, especially *Legal Guide for Starting and Running a Small*

Business,[12] *Nolo's Guide to Single-Member LLCs,*[13] and *The Employer's Legal Handbook.*[14]

---

[12] Fred S. Steingold, *Legal Guide for Starting and Running a Small Business* (Nolo Books).

[13] Fred S. Steingold, *Nolo's Guide to Single-Member LLCs* (Nolo Books).

[14] Fred S. Steingold, *The Employer's Legal Handbook* (Nolo Books).

THE RIPPLING EFFECT
OF OUR SCHOLARSHIP

According to an old Indian saying, if you give a man a fish, he eats for a day, but if you teach him to fish, he can eat for a lifetime. That is what education can do for an individual. The Nicholas J. and Mary B. Claps Scholarship 1992 at the University of Nebraska Foundation helps people obtain an education, which continues to help them throughout their lifetimes.

Our scholarship also helps parents keep more of their money for their retirement. Grandparents do not have to use their money to help their grandchildren get an education. This is the rippling effect; a scholarship helps more than the person who receives it.

Please pass this book on to others or purchase this book for any young person you know to give them a head start in life. There are many lessons here that you may have never heard or learned. Hopefully, you have found something personally useful or valuable.

The scholarship was developed with love in 1992, to make a college education available to family members and other students from our area of New York. We hope that it will continue to benefit many students for many years.

If you can, please contribute to our scholarship. Kindly send a check to:

University of Nebraska Foundation
1010 Lincoln Mall, Suite 300
Lincoln, NE 68508

Make your check payable to *University of Nebraska Foundation* and write "Nicholas J. and Mary B. Claps Scholarship dated 2/22/1992" on the memo line.

All proceeds from the sale of this book go to our scholarship.

SOME FINAL WORDS

We have learned many life lessons of value. Our goal in writing this book was to pass along some of the lessons and suggestions that worked well. What you do with them is up to you! Looking back, we asked ourselves, "How did we get here?" It is the same way you will get here. We started saving early, investing in the S&P 500 Index Fund, and letting our money grow. We are worth more than we ever dreamed as a direct result of starting to save early.

As you go through phases in your life, revisiting particular lessons or suggestions we have provided may help you navigate those phases more effectively and productively. You may even find reading the book more than once helpful as you go through different periods of your life.

Never let *anything* stand in your way—your doubts, shortcomings, handicaps, etc. Be persistent and never give up on yourself. *If anything gets in your way, it is **you**.*

The world changes faster and faster every year. As time goes on, new ideas/concepts/financial instruments come into being. Our hope is that future editions will be written by a family member or someone who has benefited from this book to update, supplement, and expand our original work.

Planning was key in making it possible for us to have the lifestyle we enjoyed, including work and leisure. With the help of this book, you can create a plan to get to the right place. If this book helps you, then it was worth our time and effort.

Acknowledgements

To my wife of over fifty years,
thank you for your support.

—NICK

To my husband,
in appreciation of our love through the years.

—MARY BETH

Connect with Nick and Mary Beth at
www.BuildingYourWealthBook.com

CPSIA information can be obtained
at www.ICGtesting.com
Printed in the USA
JSHW080845281122
33809JS00005BB/17